IF HE DON'T LOVE GOD
LOVE YOU

BRUISED BUT NOT
BROKEN

A STORY WRITTEN BY

BRENDA J

Bruised but
not Broken

Ok let's get something straight, everything that I'm writing is the truth and nothing but the truth. I was so scared to write this book at first because of what people would think about me in the end, but I came to realize that my story can help someone going through a similar predicament. In the end, it was God that allowed me to go through these things to get the glory out of what I was going through, He made a way out for me as well.

Domestic violence is real if you know someone that's going through, please call the national domestic violence hotline at 1-800-799-SAFE (7233) PLEASE! I believe if God didn't place certain people in my life at that time, I probably would have been DEAD!

Prepare yourself, for what you are about to read is going to take you on the most intense emotional roller coaster of your life. So, get your drinks and your popcorn, because this is going to be as good as any movie you have seen. Keep in mind though, that the main thing I want you to get out of this Book is how REAL God really is.

I truly want to thank God for my family and friends for encouraging me to write this book and allowing my voice to be heard. These are the questions you are going to be asking through this experience,

Who has HIV?
Wait, Who's Gay?
How did you escape?
Your father did what now?
How many baby daddies?
WHO SLEPT WITH WHO?
WHY? BRENDA NOOOO!!!

Nobody understood me growing up

Nobody understood me because, No one took the time out to ask me anything. when I was 8 years old, I was in elementary and my mom was married into a horrible family. My mom was never really around like she is now. She was either at work or the club. Now that I am a mother, I understand the sacrifices of being a mother. I use to get beat by her ex-husband for no reason. I couldn't wait for her to get home to tell her, but sometimes she didn't. We would stay with his mother for days at a time. There were times I had to wear the same clothes that I wore to school the next day because they didn't bring us any clothes. My hair was never done, there wasn't a day that I didn't get picked on by people in the school. They treated as if I was some type of disease. No one wanted to be around me, neither be my friend. Elementary school was the worst but people didn't know I was being molested the whole time at home and then I had to turn around and be mistreated at school.

He would touch me every day, he had me to do things I never thought anybody would do. I believe my mother's ex-husband mother knew what was going on, but of course she turned the other cheek as always. He would wake me up out my sleep and there were times that I would be bold enough to tell him no and he would punch me in the head, so of course I got up. I never knew a penis could go into someone's butt. I always wanted to know why a penis taste salty now that I am older, I realize it means that he wasn't clean. I hated it so much, one day when we were coming home from school, he told all of my cousins to go play hide and go seek and he did it to me as always. I never knew what cum was, all I know is that it was sticky. I never felt anything but pain. He almost got caught but he wouldn't have gotten in any trouble because come to find out that's what their family does, hide things and sleep with one another.

I never understood why he picked me out of all my cousins that were there. Writing this is making me think about a lot of things that I had to go through. I'm glad that he did something in front of my siblings, so that I would be able to have witnesses when I am brave enough to come out. After 2 years I was finally ready to come out, I couldn't take it anymore!!! I had to put a stop to it. when I finally came out, guess what? It was all my fault, boy I tell you about black families. My mom and her ex-husband asked me things to see if I can describe anything. Well I described everything to them. After that, they told me to go to bed, but her ex-husband followed me and told me I would have to leave his house because I'm trying to break up his family. He gave me a flashlight, it was around 1:00 am in the hood. I began crying because I knew where I was but my mission was to go to my grandmother on my mom side house. By the time I hit the corner he Called me to come back. My face was full of tears, I knew I shouldn't have said anything.

After that night, I never spoke on anybody else that did it to me. At the age of 11 is the age that I became a woman and didn't know. Between the ages of 8-10, I was getting penetrated in the butt and other things I had to do, but at 11 my virginity was taken from me by three of my God brothers. I was sleeping when I felt the heaviness and the motion on my body. All three of them were taking turns having they're way with me. I opened my eyes a little bit to see what was going on. I didn't want them to do anything to me if I was to panic, so I pretended like I was still asleep, but when they were finished, I opened my eyes and pulled my panties up. I asked them why did I smell like sex and they all began laughing. I went to the bathroom and cleaned myself up. When I told their mom, she said that I was lying and never to repeat it again. Of course, I didn't and now that I am grown, I see that she was trying to protect her sons. She always did more for me out of all my mama kids due to the fact that she knew I was no longer a virgin and it was all because of her grown sons who should've been locked up.

Trust me, being molested by different people didn't stop until I was 15, people wonder why at 16 I was addicted to sex. God bless the dead, I had a boyfriend and, in my mind, I was still a virgin. I was ready to have sex on my timing with some that I love so I always say I lost my virginity at 16. When I finally had sex, I thought it was going to be amazing, the way people made it seems, but honestly, I couldn't get into it. I don't know if it was him lacking in what he was packing or the things that happened to me. I didn't know that you were not supposed to tell a man that but I did and I faked it the whole time. Sex was my middle name and I ended up getting a sex partner that rocked my world. I would want it all day every day. it would be times that he couldn't take it, but the drive was so crazy. I wanted to try different people and different things. I didn't understand why I was like this, but I knew where it came from. It became so bad that I started wanting grown men. I felt like a guy my age wasn't cutting it, but in reality, I was sick and needed help. I would have sex if I was angry, happy or sad, if it's raining or if something looks sexual, I wanted it. There was a real sex demon in thriving within me. I even started having sex with females and watching other people have sex in flesh not porn.

I held so much in. I haven't told anybody, but I remember when I was in school, people would pick on me about my teeth and had no clue what I was going through. I used to pray at night that God fixed my teeth before the next morning. I had that much faith, I would get up and run to the bathroom just see if he fixed them and when I realized he didn't, I would get sad. I always cried why me God. Why did I have to be the one that goes through a lot.

After all that I had been through, I can truly say that I am grateful for everything that God is doing. He turns my bad into good, the games I played in life, getting a gun pointed at my head in the middle of nowhere from being on drugs etc. It isn't cute to be out in the streets. I had to learn the hard way. If you don't know what it feels like to be sold for drugs, then don't tell me what I should've done I was someone else property until I got away.

1 year earlier

  Most girls have this vision where they Marry the man of their dreams, have a dream house and a few kids. Not thinking about what actually comes behind it, bills, stress, fatigue and did I mention BILLS! UGHHHH! Well unfortunately, that was exactly my problem. The only difference is that I wanted the baby first, then the husband afterward. I'm not sure why but at the age of 18, I wanted my first child. I dropped out of school when I was only 16 and went back at the age of 17 and was able to graduate in my right grade. I met My first boyfriend ever in high school my freshmen year. He was 1 grade higher than me and was in the wrong class, but we wrote notes to each other, started talking, so on and so forth. We ending up dating and he was the best. He meant the world to me plus he was smart and different.

After a year we ended up moving on the west side of Jacksonville fl. I broke up with him because I began dating this guy that I met at church, but I told him it was because of the distance and we wouldn't be able to see each other. Fast forward a few years later, I ran into him on the city bus in Jacksonville fl. We spoke and he was telling me all the successful things he accomplished like him attending college at UF which he wasn't lying about, AND OF COURSE, I made up a story because I didn't want him to know that I was a stripper. we ended up reconnecting and he was crazy about me once again. He invited me to stay at his dorm and he gave me any and everything I wanted, not knowing he as using his student loans. Now to really seal the deal, he was a virgin & I wasn't. I mean we used to dry hunch but it wasn't anything major. So, one night I asked him was he ready and he quickly replied yes. You know from that point on, I had to teach him a few things.

things took a turn for the worst after that. He wanted me to stay even longer. He wasn't going to school, He was starting to get careless, and he asked me to marry him. Of course, I said yes. He immediately called his mom and she wasn't feeling it at all. fast forward some after that, I left and just dropped him, and he lost EVERYTHING, he had to moved back with his mom, he couldn't find a job, he was kicked out of school, the whole 9 yards. So of course, we reconnected and I am still the only woman that he ever slept with. He wanted more and I wanted the baby and him. We ended up having sex one day and he didn't pull out on time. I was happy but didn't want to show it so I just shrugged it off like "Oh well". A week later, I started talking about baby names and he was not interested at all. I took the bus to get a pregnancy test because I wasn't coming on my period. I took the test in the dollar tree bathroom and it came out to be positive. OH MY GOD!!! I was so happy and couldn't wait to tell him. I called and told him, he was quiet, so quiet that you could hear a pen drop. after that, I didn't hear from him. He wouldn't pick up my calls or anything. It just so happened, I was going to meet my sugar daddy, I finally seen him and when I tell y'all I was eated, I was so angry. I literally snapped on him and all. I was so scared to tell my parents. I went to bed worrying and stressing trying to figure out a way to tell my mom, next thing I know, I began having unbearable sharp pains, but I ignored them because I wanted my baby. A week passed and I am still cramping really bad and now I'm bleeding. It's getting to the point that I can't bare it anymore. So, I had a neighbor take me because I didn't want my parents to know, I called him and told it all. he gave his mom some bull crap story about his friend being there because he broke his arm but it was me losing my baby. Somehow my parents found out and was trying to come to the hospital, but we both was ignoring them. When the doctor said "ma'am the test is still positive but u just had miscarriage" tears immediately started falling. This is only the beginning.

What's a Father Figure

A few months passed and I was laying down thinking about my older sister on my dad side. I wanted to know what was she like. Out of the blue I decided to check my messenger and noticed that she inboxed me I haven't spoke to her since I was 10. I messaged her back and she gave me her number. we talked for hours on end. She ended up telling me that our father was out of prison. she ended up giving him my number and he called me the same day and told me he wanted me to come to Tallahassee, FL but something kept telling me not to, but I thought to myself "what if he's dying, I don't want to regret not seeing him" so he booked me a ticket for the greyhound, I was so nervous. I haven't seen him since I was 10. I don't even remember what he looks like. I mean I always wanted to know him. He's never really been in my life and I wanted to know where I came from. I made it to the bus station safely in, but I didn't know where he was coming from, So I sat and waited, he finally came and he didn't look like any of the pictures I seen when I was younger, but I have to remember that he was diagnosed with HIV when he went to prison for sleeping with men, but from what I was told he went to prison for having sex with children (boys) back in the 90s and someone from prison raped him and gave it to him, but he looks as if he wasn't taking his meds. He hugged me when he noticed me and there was this guy with him that caught my eye. He was really cute with dreads, smooth skin, AND he was a smooth talker. Honey he was fine! So, my dad's friend put my bags in the car. I should've known he was both ways due to the fact that he hung out with my father, but you know, I didn't know any better. When we arrived to my sister's house, my dad friend took my things into her apartment. I whispered to my dad and told him "he was cute" he was like "you should talk to him". My sister and I were so happy to see each other, my niece had gotten so big. A month passed and the guy and I started talking, but we stopped when found out that he lied about his identity, everything about him was a lie and when I found out him and my dad was sleeping together that was a wrap for me, but he still wanted to be with me. My dad did all that he could to keep us apart. I am so glad we were just talking and didn't jump into anything. His looks were everything but mentally, he wasn't stable. I attended this church in tally and the apostle that was there told me that there was a man that was going to walk in my house and he means me no good. I was so confused because the only guy I thought about was the guy I stop talking to.

How I met the enemy

My dad brought this guy over to help bring up the TV that he got for my sister at the thrift store. My dad   always had somebody with him, he was never alone. My dad and I were talking while my sister and the guy were talking up in her room as he put the TV together. Knowing me, I played bougie of course because I knew my body was banging and my makeup was on fleek, he was low-key staring at me, but I was ignoring him. I was basically trying to push him onto my sister. I was trying to get me a college dude out here. They all came in the living room and began talking, I wasn't really saying anything.

 My dad ended up inviting him over for thanksgiving since he didn't really have family here. The day of thanksgiving, he decided to have conversation with me. I mean he was cool and smooth. He brought up the dude and how they ended fighting because he brought my name up. that kind of turn me on. I felt the vibe of him pushing me away, but that made me want him even more. I had never been rejected.

 We ended up talking almost every single day. Day and night, he ended up going out of town around Christmas, but brought me back a promise ring. I thought he was lying until my dad gave it to me, I didn't care if it was stolen or not, knowing that he doesn't have a job, but I cherished it. I asked for some explicit pictures and honey when I tell u I asked him "can I have some" and he started laughing. I used to pick him up every day. Remind you, sex offenders that are on probation have a curfew. I was really feeling him to. I just knew that he was the one, or was it because he had a big penis? I only knew him for a month in a half and we ended up bringing the new year's together. Child he was mines.

Terrible Beginnings

WARNING SEX SEX SEX
 I haven't had sex in forever and I think it's about that time for me to see what he can offer, knowing I was a freak. So, when we went in the room, we started kissing, but I stopped to go ask my sister for a condom. Oh, you thought were going raw? You can tell he couldn't wait to taste me. I watched him as he put on the condom. He put it in from behind and I melted. I never felt so much pleasure all at once, now this is what you called sex. I noticed he pulled out for a second. So, I turned around and saw him struggling to put the condom back on and that's when I realized that he snuck the condom off and he went in raw the whole time. Then that's when I said "you already went in raw, you might as well finish". So, he went deeper and deeper I screamed so loud and cried out with pleasure. After we were done, I asked him "How could you trust going in me raw like that when you don't even know me?" But what I should've asked myself is "why would you let him go in raw when you don't even know him?" After that day, we had sex every day at least 3 times a day. My sex drive for him was crazy! I started to noticed my sister was getting a bit jealous of our relationship. She would catch an attitude but

her baby daddy was released from prison. I guess she wasn't satisfied with him sexually. Not to mention he ask me to have a threesome with them. He even busted in the room on us having sex just so he can get some type of peek at me.

Anyways her attitude definitely did a full 360 and I really couldn't understand why. He came home from work and I would have his bath water and food ready as always. My mom kept telling me to stop having sex until you are married, and she was right. I know who God is and I being extremely disobedient. I told him that it was better to marry then to burn and that we could no longer have sex until we were married. So, guess what happened after that? That's right, we decided to get married. We order our rings off amazon and he proposed the same day quit my job at sonics.

Now to refresh your memory, we literally just met in the end of November and were married in March. You do the math. Thing became so bad with my sister that we had to move out when she found out we got married, not knowing my dad was throwing stuff at both us, I found out he told her that I called DCF on her. I was so shocked. We ended up moving in with this lady until we could get our own. I was waiting on my student loans to come through so I could use it to get us our own place. He ended up losing his job so I was making him a resume and he ended up getting a really good job soon after.

I started praying more and I found a place where he was able to register by him being a sex offender. I found out it was a lot of sex offenders out there. I was able to use my student loan to pay for the down payment and the 1st months' rent. We ended up getting lights in his name. Our first night was unbelievable, we seriously couldn't believe it. We soon realized it was too many roaches in there. That same night we had to go to the store to get some bombs and never had a problem again. My thrifting senses began tingling and I found so many things on craigslist and Facebook. We ended up getting some pretty good furniture. The people that work with women had me to pick out some things I wanted. I got a nice couch, dining set, basically the whole nine ards, only thing missing was my 40 acres and a mule. When I was finished, the house was fully furnished. He went to work and every day he came home to a bath, a hot meal and his beer and cigarettes. 2 months in our place and the nightmare is about to take place.

get out or die? the choice is yours

He finally came home I believe it was probably around 3:00 am, and he was looking for me. He sat in front down in front of me and I can tell he was some pretty heavy drugs because his eyes were not the same. He was giving me a speech on how he was tired of living like this. He pulled out a knife and pointed it at my stomach. Tears rapidly began falling down my face. When he realized that I feared him, he moved and left. Now I realize it's either get out or I'm going to die with my baby. So, I put on some clothes, called the police and they came and picked me up. They took him to the psyche ward for 24 hours. I remember him telling me a long time ago that if I ever called the police on him, he would kill me and then let the police kill him. I called this prophet that I knew and she had me to call the domestic violence hotline. I was scared for my life. I packed a couple things up and the police took me to shelter. I felt so hopeless and confused when I went in there, but it was a private place to keep women and children safe from there abusive husband. What I didn't tell y'all was that he didn't start beating on me until I was pregnant. I still use to cover for him. One time, I literally had to run out of the house naked because of it. he was mentally, physically and emotionally abusing me. I didn't want anybody to talk about me, so I just sat there and took it. I wanted to call my old sugar daddy to send for me, but he honestly hated my guts for leaving him to stay even after everything that I just said. I just wanted to get away for a few days, he completely cut me off!!!! I walked in the place confused and scared. I had to sleep in a room with another family I kind of still talk to til this day. When I finally realized that he was out, I called him, but he wouldn't answer my calls. I felt bad because I loved him and I wanted to make it work no matter what, so I called him on the place phone and it calls restricted and he answered. He was begging me to come home. Part of me wanted to, but part of me didn't. I knew the lies wouldn't stop, the abuse, I couldn't think of what I wanted, it was about my baby. So, I've been there about a week now. I'm not stupid, I'm pretty sure he's been cheating on me, but honestly this place helped me so much. My case worker at the program spoke to me. She helped me get into this pregnancy homeless shelter, honestly, you might as well say it was the bad girls club, but we were pregnant. It was a very beautiful home.

Everyone had their own room, 2 people had to share a bathroom and the kitchen was really big. OH MY GOSH! and there were 4 refrigerators. Me and him still weren't on good terms honestly. I called him every day and he was too focused on the drugs and women, he didn't care anything about my baby and I. It was as if he was free. Before I moved to the pregnancy shelter, I ended up going to the computer lab and something told me to go through his emails. The things that I saw were hurt me beyond any of your imaginations. I SCREAMED TO THE TOP OF MY LUNGS, I WAS ON ON THE FLOOR CRYING. My case worker came in and asked what was wrong? Why was I screaming and crying? All I could say was "HE'S GAY! HE BEEN SLEEPING WITH MEN ALL THIS TIME!" All the emails proved it. The pictures, the men that he met off of craigslist. I just felt like I died. I ended calling him that same night and he owned up to it. He couldn't lie because I had all the proof. I knew he was going to change his password, so I forwarded the messages to myself. I settled down at the pregnancy shelter after knowing all of that, I still wanted him. sexual demons are so real. They will make you think its love, but honestly the foundation was built off of lust.

A baby can't keep a man

My ex-husband was at work and I was sitting home. I asked my neighbor to take me to the store to pick him up some cigarettes and beer before he came home. The food was already done, she looked at me and asked "are you pregnant?" I told her "no ma'am". I didn't think anything of it because I just had a miscarriage not too long ago, but it came back to my attention that I had been really sick for the past 2 nights. So, I picked up two pregnancy tests. I was very hesitant when it came down to actually taking the test, but I finally did and they both came out positive. I called him while he was on the roof working and he was ecstatic. He couldn't work because he couldn't believe that he was having a baby again. Now when I say again, I am referring to his ex that gave his baby up for adoption when he was sent to prison.

When he came home, he gave me a kiss and he was rubbing my stomach. I told him that I already picked the names and he agreed to them. I became so sick that I literally had to drop out of college because I couldn't do anything! 2 months passed and I was sick every single day. He would come home pissed off, not wanting to touch me at all and complaining. it became so bad, that he wouldn't come home until 1 sometimes 2 in the morning, if not, later than that. Sometimes I would lock him out because no one comes in my home after 12.

Now remind you, this is the same man I opened up to and told my deepest darkest secrets. I remember us laying in the bed, sharing stories we both know we will have to take to our graves.

I told him how I was molested by my cousins, how my body was sold for drugs by a couple who had me doped up in south Florida, how I was taken to the woods with a gun pointed at my head, how I was addicted to sex from being touched by grown men, I kept it a secret for so many years, flocka is a terrible drug and I was smoking it unknowingly. I even told him during my stripping days that I was raped in the club and went back the next day. I even told him how I thought about killing myself due to the lack of love, I even told him how I used to be jealous of my little sister. I told him my fears. I thought I was doing that because a wife is supposed to be open with her husband, but in reality, he was taking notes to use against me. mentally, physically and emotional.

A month later

He came home late and drunk as always, I always thought that when a person does that, they are trying to escape from reality. I come from a very spiritual family and I'm what you would call a dreamer. God gave me a dream that my husband at the time was sleeping with two women at the same time. Now I know some of you are saying to yourselves "OK so god showed you that he is cheating on you with two different women" but that wasn't the case. If you didn't know, Dreams are always the opposite of what you dreamt. What I'm about to tell you is going to break it all down for you. I was a bit confused and I thought to myself "I really must be tripping.... yeah that's it, I'm just tripping" or so I thought. Something told me to go through his phone, which is something I don't do. I found pictures of a man's butt that he saved from craigslist. I wish y'all could've seen how fast I got up. He was out cold next to me and I screamed to the top of my lungs "Nigga you gay and u didn't tell me!" I was punching him in his chest and he finally grabbed and told me "no baby somebody had my phone" blah blah just lying, but honestly, I believed him, but there was a voice in the back of my mind that kept saying he was lying. I decided to play it off because I didn't want my daughter to feel any of that. I always wanted a mini me but anyways, that's besides the point.

I decided to look his name up on facebook and I ran across his old profile that he had way before he went to prison and he shared a video of men twerking. I shook my head and asked him about it. He told me that they were just having fun with their friends. I said what grown man watch another grown man twerk? But once again I looked over it. ALL OF THE SIGNS WERE THEIR BRENDA!

I decided to put on my thinking cap. I remember being in my dad's room with my ex husband and his friend. We were planning on watching a movie. We turned the TV on and it was a video of two men doing.... you know what. knowing my dad, the Bishop of the church, I was so surprised even though I knew that he was gay, but it was the reaction that his friend gave me that my ex-husband didn't. Once again, I decided to overlook it. He ended up losing his job, or so he says. He was laid off, but I still believe that it was much more to it than that. He started hanging out with the drug heads that stayed in the complex, one day we needed rent and I had some money stashed for rainy days as every woman should. He told me he needed to flip it to pay our bills, so he went and purchased some supplies. I asked him "where was the money that you were supposed to flip" he told me "I couldn't get rid of it" but I seen him go back and fourth getting supplies.

I was so angry at myself for being so stupid. Now we don't have any money for bills, but little did he know, I've been paying the rent up behind his back just in case he decided to leave me. I was pregnant and /*miserable. He would come home high and drunk, wanting to get on top of me but I would always reject him. Some nights he would just take it and I would just lay there until he was done. he would scream "You are MY wife, I can take it whenever I want to. I felt so helpless. I had no one to tell or turn to but God. I even felt as if God hated me. When he left to get high late at night, sometimes I would ball up in a corner and cry. I remember one night, he left and I took some bleach, poured it in the tub with hot water and grabbed a knife. I was really going to slit my wrist. I was ready to end it all. I was tired of the pain, the suffering and felt like this was my only way out, but before I was able to slit my wrist, he grabbed me and took the knife, then he left again I COULDN'T TAKE IT ANYMORE! That's when reality hit me, I'm pregnant with my baby girl, so I just prayed and stayed up until he came home.

"Why do I still want him?" that was a thought that I had while I sat in the bed. It was comfortable even though it was a twin bed. I thought about the time I started smoking cigarettes because of the stress. Yes, I was pregnant and selfish, but he put some drugs in my cigarette one time and I was lying on him and I asked him "babe why does it feel like I'm floating?" He just started laughing and told me what he did. I was so confused because I told him that I get very paranoid whenever I smoke, that's why I don't smoke. That's why you have to be careful what you tell people, seriously. I finally decided to call him but he didn't answer, So I played my gospel music and balled up and started crying, begging God to save my marriage, knowing it was over. I ended up getting a job at Wendy's down the street. I had a plan for myself. I got so tired of walking and standing up long, so I had to leave the job. Both of our birthdays were in August, so I decided to cook for him, take it to him and go fishing. Even after everything I found out, I still wanted to be with him and I just couldn't understand it because he still treated me like crap. 2

days later, it was my birthday and the homeless shelter allows you to leave on the weekends, but you must get permission. I decided to go home for a few days. When I arrived, I unlocked the door and he wasn't home. Now I need you guys to understand that I didn't have a car, so I took the city bus. I had to take 3 buses just to get there. I walked in and it was stank and in a mess. I went in our room and found a jacket that I have never seen before, I checked the pockets and found a condom and my heart immediately dropped.

He came home and I asked him "who's jacket is this?" Then he told me that it was the neighbors. So, I asked the neighbor and he told me that it wasn't his. The wife said that's not his or hers. She was throwing hints that someone had been in my house. He snapped on me. Of course, I let it go, but deep down inside, I was so hurt, I knew no one would want me. I was big and pregnant. We ended up going to this couple's party that we knew in the same complex. Everyone was high and drunk except for me. I started dancing and he almost broke my neck when he realized what I was doing. I looked at him and asked "you can do it, but I can't?" I watched him watch this one guy all night long.

We ended up going to this old man house that we knew that he does drugs with. He was the biggest liar that you will ever meet but he was cool people. god bless the dead. Him and some other guys started smoking, but what made me sick is when he started doing cocaine right in front me and allowed other people to smoke crack while I was in the room even though I was pregnant, but of course he didn't care. I decided to go through his phone while he was doing all of that and I saw porn, now if you have made it this far then you should already know what kind of porn he was watching. If you don't know, it was gay porn. I began crying and he knew why, so he snatched his phone and grabbed my arm and drug me all the way back to our apartment. He was cussing me out, of course. Next day comes and we are sitting in the house, I'm starving, it was hotter than fish grease in that house, our lights were turned off, the house was horrendously filthy, you could tell that he did not take care of our place, I had to sleep on the floor because I gave one of the girls my furniture due to the fact that I wasn't staying there, oh yeah, can't forget the fact that I'm pregnant. He ended falling asleep but I kept waking him up, begging for food and water but he just refused to give me anything. I was hot, nauseous and I was throwing up stomach acid. I finally got up and went outside. I saw a lady smoking and I begged her for water. She gave it to me. When he finally came outside, he seen me and pulled me back into the house. He told me that I better not leave again. He went back to sleep and I grabbed a real old phone that he hid from me for so long and guess what I found? I bet you thought it was more gay porn, didn't you? Well no, it wasn't. I found message after message, pictures of men sending to him, they're meet up spots, EVERYTHING! I just kept telling myself "enough is enough." I decided to sit on the porch and cry. Two men were sitting in a truck and they kept asking was I OK, but I didn't answer. but here he comes and his exact words were "Brenda if you don't get in here, I will kill you" So I went back in and laid down. I knew he was cheating because not once has he touched me while he was high and drunk. I kept waking him, asking him over and over again, "do you love me?" He didn't respond. So, I asked him again and he woke up yelling "NO! Since you want to ask dumb questions. "I couldn't take anymore" is what I told myself. Even though my older sister did what she did, I was in need of her help.

The escape

It's now or never, so I decided to text my older sister and I told her everything. She was willing to help me. She had already moved back to Jacksonville FL and you can tell she was a little hesitant because I would always claim that I was going to leave but I didn't. At this moment I was dead serious, when a woman fed up, SHE IS FED UP! trust me. I decide to break my plan down to her. The plan was to wake up in the morning, make him think that I was going back to the shelter, call the shelter and let them know that I was planning on moving back, pack all the things that I could fit in my suitcase, hop on the greyhound and get the hell out of dodge, never to look back. while doing all of that, I had to somehow convince him to think that I was still in Tallahassee.

Every time it looks like he's about to get up, I play sleep until I hear this certain snore that he does. I went back to texting her and she went on ahead and booked my ticket. she said "Brenda if you don't come, I will never do anything else for you." I told her that I'm serious this time. The sun comes up and of course, I haven't slept. He woke up and went outside. I began gathering my things to get ready to leave. I finally walked outside where I see him talking to his druggie friends. He noticed that I was packed and ready to go. He decided to walk me to the bus stop. We haven't really said anything to each other but once the bus pulled up, I told him bye. He said "what's that supposed to mean?" I said "good bye" once again. I believe that he thought I was bluffing. Once I was on the bus, I began making phone calls. I believe the shelter thought that I was going back to him, so they watched my every move. The director even suggested that she would drop me off. She stayed with me up until she seen me print off my ticket. That's when she gave me some money to put in my pocket. I sat there eating my meal, it was just so hard to believe that I am almost free. I called him and talked to him as if nothing was happening. I believe that he knew something was going on, but he didn't realize it.

My final bus pulled up and that was my door opening to my freedom. I didn't believe it until I arrived in Jacksonville. All I could do was cry. I am no longer a prisoner to that evil man. My sister ended up picking me up and taking me back to her place. I was miserable and depressed the entire time. I ended up calling my mom after a week of being in Jacksonville. I told her that I was back. I told her everything that I wanted her to know. Eventually I ended up moving in with my mother until she helped me get into my own place. I haven't found a doctor yet, but I ended up getting my own place after only a month, my house was fully furnished and my daughter had everything she needed. He still believes that I was in Tallahassee until he seen where I was. he was so angry and was begging for me to let him move in with me. I told him that he could after the baby shower due to the fact that my mom told me if I was to bring him into my place, she would cut me off. I told him to wait until Saturday. Why am I taking him back? I don't know, maybe it was love. I guess I went through all of that to get away for me to bring him back here with me, But God had other plans.

PERMANENT DAMAGE

I finally found a doctor. I haven't seen my daughter in what feels like an eternity. I couldn't believe that I was about to a mother. We were deep at the place. They ended up taking a blood and a glucose test. I hated it since I had to sit there for an hour and I was starving. It was my sister on my mother's side, my dad and my mom. The next day I was at home of course on the phone with him and I started coughing. He asked me why was I coughing like that? I said that it was probably a cold or something. The way he asked made me think like "Uh OK." The nurse ended up calling me saying that they needed to see me ASAP. I asked "for what?" She said Mrs. Henry, I really need to see you. I ended up calling my mom and told her that I was a little worried at first and she told not to worry about it. I knew what she didn't know, that my ex-husband sleeps with men. I asked him "is there something that he needs to tell me before tomorrow?" He told me no. Of course, my dumb behind believed him. My mom came to get me and took me to the doctor's office. We got called in the back and I started to feel nauseous due to the fact we went to the opposite side of that doctor's office and the wall had different diseases posted on the wall. The doctor finally came in and she asked did I want my mom in the room? I told my mom to step out just in case it was bad, I want to swallow that pill by myself first. My mom stepped out and the doctor said so much without actually saying what she wanted to say. She finally told me "your blood came back positive for HIV"

I screamed at the top of my lungs. I was screaming and crying. My mom asked me what was going on and the doctor told her. I held my mom and all I could say is "mom I'm too young to die! How could he do this to me? I'm only 19, he would've left me alone. The doctor told me everything I needed to know to protect me and my baby. We were leaving and my mom was so quiet.

You can tell she was trying to be strong for me, but she wanted to cry. I had to call my sister and dad, my sister cried and my dad (My mother's husband) was quiet but he was hurt he just tried not to show it. When we got to my mom's house, you can tell my mom was crying her eyes out. My mom showed me this young lady who was open about her status. She came over to talk to me and encouraged to get the police involved. I decided to, but first I wanted to hear from him. I called him and he answered. I asked him do you know I have HIV? His response was "NO... NO baby, I knew something was wrong with me." I said "listen, the damage has already been done, you might as well tell me the truth." He said that he knew for years that he was positive. He didn't want to tell me because he didn't want to lose me. All I could think "was I going to die?" I had to get the police involved, especially after I found that the mother before me is also positive. She found out when she gave birth. Then she gave the baby up for adoption. He hated her for that but now it all make since.

THE TRUTH HAS SPREAD

After everything that I found out, secret after secret, I found out that he lied about why he went to prison as sex offender, he lied about how many kids he had, he lied about pretty much everything you can think of. The crazy thing is that my sperm donor knew all about it. He knew that he was gay and positive but he didn't care, he's the one that married us. He only did it to get back at my mom. He knew that if he couldn't get her, the next to a woman is her child. My own sperm donor told me that if he could live with it, then so can I. Yes, I had him locked up a few days after I had my daughter. The police finally found him. Someone called the tip line, thank God! I don't want him to hurt anyone else. He called me while he was in jail, his plan was to manipulate me to not talk against him and it almost worked. I almost fell for everything he told me. I still claimed him due to the fact that I wasn't mentally stable. I was so embarrassed. I thought that I could hide it from the world but unfortunately the world found out due to it making it to the news. People noticed that it was my ex-husband and they were inboxing me saying that they were sorry. All I could do was cry, it got to the point that the article ended up on Facebook. People were bashing me. I finally told my sperm donor that I knew he slept with my ex-husband. All he did was hang up the phone in my face. New Year's came in for 2017 and the prophet told me that if I go back that I would die, meaning that he would kill me.

We meet again

It's around August when I reconnected with my high school sweet heart. Yes, I know I'm beginning to look dumb at this point. I mean he lied about so much, but at this point in my life, I just didn't care. I needed attention and love from someone. I knew that he didn't love me or anything, but remember, I'm still the first only woman that he has ever slept with. I'm basically offering my him my body for attention and company. He does know about my status but he didn't care. I honestly told him that I think I am ready for another baby due to the fact that I felt like another child would help me love myself. You could tell that he wasn't really feeling it, but he still didn't want to use any protection with me, he never pleased me whatsoever. I just wanted someone there, a man I should say. I knew for sure that no man was going to want me knowing that I'm a single mother with an infected vagina, but honestly, I wasn't look at how god would bless me with my own, and the fact that I'm not detected, meaning that I can't pass it to anyone that I connect with.

He ended up taking me out for my birthday, I'm finally 21. I decided to get a drink. Since I don't really drink, I ended up getting my favorite, sex on the beach with extra orange juice. I was tipsy not even 5 minutes in. We ended up getting a hotel room. We began talking about why he ended up joining the military, knowing he was against it. He kept me updated about his life. Now remind you I seen him before I left to go to Tallahassee. He was giving me the update about him going to UF. I believed him because he had proof and he asked me what did I do. I told him that I was in college, but to be honest, I was a stripper who was making money. I knew I had the body for it. I just knew I wasn't on his level and I will never be even though he is a liar.

A month later, I've been feeling a title weird. My little sister (even though we are only a year apart) ended up going to family dollar with me. She told me to take a pregnancy test. I ended up taking it in the bathroom to find out that I was pregnant. I was honestly happy, but I know for a fact that he was going to flip. I really didn't care, I got what I wanted. Of course, he ran away and I haven't spoken to him since found out. I looked at it as I have my 2 babies and I wanted a boy. God blessed me with another girl I'm sure I know why but I'm grateful. I ran into his mother and I decided to be petty. I told her everything. She said that he talked so bad about me, she would've never imagined that I would be pregnant with his baby. I let it go because the entire family were snakes. I HAD TO CUT HIM OFF COMPLETELY! I went through a really bad depression. I wasn't bathing or cleaning. I was still talking to my ex-husband, putting money on the phone and receiving letters. I felt so lonely. If only you guys would've seen how I would be at the mail box. You might as well have called me Celie from the color purple. I would ask the mail lady did anything come for me, now looking back at that, I looked pathetic. My mom had to come over to clean and bathe me. She even prayed for me and she honestly prayed me out of depression. I vent to church one night and this man of God told me not to receive another letter, not knowing that my ex-husband did witchcraft. Every time I received a letter from him, I would get depressed and just want to die, but I had to stop because I have a little girl to live for and another one on the way.

a year later

was laying on my couch and I told myself that I was bored. I remember an app I used to get on when I was younger. It was a dating website and decided to sign up again. Honestly, every dude that inboxed me went straight to the blocked list. I wasn't looking for anything, I was just bored, but there was this one guy though that really caught my attention. In his profile picture, he had his finger in his nose and all I could say was he's weird and different. He almost reminds me of my ex who passed away. He was dark skinned and handsome, so I inboxed him. was short texting him though. I was ready to delete the app. I told him that I was and he was like "Well, let me get your number before you get off and I was like "I don't know" I gave him a text now number just in case he didn't make the cut. I ended up loving talking to him. Have you ever got this feeling that it was too good to be true? Well that's exactly ow I was feeling. We would talk on the phone for hours and hours. He was sweet, humble, handsome, and had a good job. My plan was to make him fall in love with me before I told him my status because I was afraid of what he would say, but I stopped myself because I knew what it felt like to be taken advantage of. that is what you call manipulation. I decided to tell him everything about me. I was so nervous before we get deeper into this. Once I told him he became silent for a second, and what he said next stills shocks me, then he said "Brenda, I still want to be with you." I cried, why did I cry? Because I always said "who will be with me knowing I have bad blood now?" Plus, I know people who are walking around even though they are undetected, are sleeping with people and not telling them.

We went on our first date. I wanted waffle house. By me being pregnant I knew the baby had to eat. After we got our food, we ate outside of his barber while we ate. Then he went in after we were done to get his haircut. I took my daughter to the hospital because I needed call out papers. After we left the hospital, I went to pick him up from the barber. We ended up going to lunch, talked some more, then he had to go to work. I haven't been on a date in I don't know how long now, I was on cloud 9. Y'all just don't understand, after the mental and emotional roller coaster I had to go through to finally be able to be my age, I thought being with an older man would satisfy my needs, but of course it didn't. Older men take advantage of young women because they know they are weak. now I understand why my mother's husband (the man that I look up to) said "What does a grown man want with my 19-year-old daughter? I didn't get it until now, but anyways his name is Brandon, he's 6'2, chocolate with beautiful teeth. now my teeth are not perfect but I can't date a man unless he has perfect teeth. He is both book smart and street smart. We talked every day and decided to go on another date. After that, we made it official. We were dating. He met my family and they loved him. He met my uncle and aunt and if you know me, you will know that know I am surrounded by real prophets. My aunt is the one that said this is the one. then it reminded me of when she told me that God is going to send me a man who going to love me for me and my children. He went to all of my infection disease doctors' appointments and he was there through all of my ups and downs, he was there through my entire pregnancy and he takes care of both of our children as if they are his blood. He is all Elizabeth and Isabella knows. A year later on December 19th, he asked me to marry him and on December 22 we became husband and wife. I never knew I had it in me to be able to trust a man but I don't just have any man, I have the man that God made especially just for me and only me.

Husband's perspective

OK! Now it's my turn. Hello I'm the editor and husband of Brenda J. Now I'm going to give you guys my side of the story and my perspective, so which one do y'all want first? Doesn't matter because I'm about to give you my side to the story. So, this is how it began. I was at work and it just so happens that it was time for me to go on break. I got in the break room and I checked my phone. I see messages coming to my POF account. I checked them and it was this short, brown skinned beauty trying to take my innocence. Little did she know, I wasn't a so easy. You have to wine and dine me first. I'm just kidding, I told her about a little restaurant that I still haven't taken her to. She always brings it up, but anyway, she was trying to play hard to get but I hit her with that smooth talk like (deep voice)"we should meet up sometimes for a little date." Now she tried to delete the app before I got the number but I wasn't going for it. I can say that since I met this beautiful woman of god, my life has done a complete turnaround. I am extremely proud of you for everything that that you have accomplished. You have broken out of your comfort zone and did everything that you set out to do. I love you and keep up the good work. Many blessings are coming your way.

Final Draft from Brenda J

I am bruised but not broken. from being dragged while I was pregnant, being starved and begging for attention, been infected by someone evil. Losing my older sister due to jealousy. In reality, God told me himself to cut her off 30 minutes before the new year's kicked in 2017, from being betrayed by the man who helped create me. From being mistreated by the complex when they had no clue what happened to me.

After all of that I went through I am still standing and it's by the grace of God. I thought I was going to die but he changed my mindset, he gave me two healthy baby girls and a husband that's negative. He blessed me with a 3-bedroom home, my own car, my own business. I STILL HAVE MY MIND!!!!!!!!! THROUGH ALL OF THAT GOD ALLOWED ME TO KEEP MY MIND. BUT GOD. BUT GOD. BUT GOD. GOD IS REAL I COULD HAD BEEN DEAD

UPDATE:

EX Husband: 4 Years in prison

REAL FATHER: Remaining as a bishop in Tallahassee still sleeping with men. but every witch shall? read the word

Brandon (Current): My husband is now an editor a deacon in training, a business owner and much more. soon to be author.

Brenda J: I am now a business owner, author and teacher. as long as I got king Jesus, I will become the woman of God that he called me to be.

THE END
Please leave reviews Thank you!
Please contact or follow me
Iambrendaj0@gmail.com
Instagram: Iambrendaj_
snapchat: nessa21